The Livingston Lion

The Livingston Lion

Henry Beekman Livingston's Revolution

Geoff Benton

Epigraph Books
Rhinebeck, New York

The opinions and statements herein are those of the author only and do not represent the opinions or interests of The Office of Parks, Recreation and Historic Preservation.

Paperback ISBN 978-1-954744-36-3
eBook ISBN 978-1-954744-37-0

Library of Congress Control Number 2021917460

Book design by Colin Rolfe

Epigraph Books
22 East Market Street, Suite 304
Rhinebeck, NY 12572
(845) 876-4861
epigraphps.com

This book is dedicated to my parents,
who took me to every historical site we could find
and opened this whole can of worms.

Contents

Introduction

For a family as well documented as the Livingston family of New York, it seems odd that any of facet of their lives would escape the search of historians. Yet Henry Beekman Livingston seems to burst onto the scene a grown man of twenty-five years.

What is known about his youth is very limited. Henry Beekman Livingston, sometimes called Harry, was born in 1750, the second son and fifth child of Judge Robert R. Livingston and his wife Margaret Beekman Livingston. Their marriage had united the Livingstons of Clermont and the Beekmans of Dutchess County, as well their large landholdings in the Hudson Valley and elsewhere that amounted to approximately one million acres of land. The couple had eleven children, ten of whom lived to adulthood. Henry was named after his maternal grandfather, Colonel Henry Beekman. In addition to being the owner of huge tracts of land, Henry Beekman was a very powerful politician in the State of New York, serving in the New York General Assembly for thirty-four years.

Henry Beekman Livingston and his siblings were born members of New York's elite. Their paternal great-grandfather Robert Livingston, the first Livingston in America, arrived in New York in 1676, just after the colony had been transferred back to the English from the Dutch for the last time. He was the youngest son of a Scottish minister who had been exiled to Rotterdam following a falling out with King Charles II of England. This put him in a perfect position to use his natural talents and his mastery of English and Dutch to take full advantages of the opportunities presented by the Dutch/English colony.

Within a decade, Robert Livingston ("the Elder") had been granted Livingston Manor and the title of Lord of the Manor. In just a few short years, he had gone from being a nearly penniless immigrant to one of the wealthiest men in the colony. That wealth would guarantee his descendants a high place in the social strata of New York for generations to come.

The manor was 160,000 acres, a legacy that Robert would split between his two surviving sons. At his death in 1728, the larger portion of the manor and his title went to the elder son Philip, while

13,000 acres of land went to the son who was named for him, Robert.

Over the course of the next ten years, son Robert built a Georgian-style mansion, which he dubbed Clermont, on a high bluff overlooking the Hudson River. At the same time, he began to buy up parcels of land on the west side of the river so that by the time he was ready to move into the house, he owned nearly 500,000 acres of land, or almost everything he could see from the front door.

This Robert's only child was a son he, too, in turn named Robert—who eventually became Judge Robert R. Livingston. The Judge's marriage nearly doubled the family's land holding. The type of wealth and power Judge Robert R. and Margaret Beekman Livingston and their children held is nearly unimaginable. They summered at Clermont and wintered in New York City. Private tutors taught them languages, classics, and other subjects. Three of their sons—Robert, John, and Edward—attended college, but there is no evidence that their fourth son Henry did.

Henry's brothers would play a variety of roles in the Revolutionary War. Robert, the eldest, was a member of Congress, helped draft the Declaration of Independence, and served as Secretary for Foreign

Affairs. John was a merchant who spent much of the war in Boston buying and selling goods for the Continental Army. He also operated gunpowder mills to supply the army, the first of which was built by his father in 1775 and was the first gunpowder mill in New York. The youngest son Edward was too young to take an active part in the war but did have to flee from the approaching British army in 1777 and in the waning days of the war spent time in the Continental Army camp. He became a favorite of the Marquis de Lafayette, who offered to take him back to France with him for a European education.

Henry, unlike his brothers, was a soldier. More specifically, he was a fighting soldier. On the battlefield Henry was a force to be reckoned with, displaying bravery and valor in every action he participated in. He fought behind enemy lines, he fought outnumbered and nearly overwhelmed—situations in which other men would blanche. He snatched victory from the jaws of defeat on several occasions. He pushed his men hard and expected the best not only out of them but also out of himself and his superiors.

Henry had all the makings of a stereotypical Revolutionary War soldier. His only prior military experience was in the colonial militia; he was brave and maybe even a little reckless in battle. He could be remembered as a self-made soldier along the lines of Henry Know or Nathanael Greene. Unlike these men, though, Henry had a personality that forever held him back.

In camp between battles, Henry was prone to disagreements with his fellow officers, which resulted in several court martials and at least one challenge to a duel. He was quarrelsome and stubborn. His attitude often swung wildly between high temper and melancholy. When he did not have an English enemy to fight, he often sought another enemy among the officers of his own side. All in all, he was a thoroughly unpleasant man to be around when he did not have a sword in his hand. Henry was also perpetually jealous of the rank of other men. He strove to raise his own rank and complained when other men were promoted around him. He could be petty to the edge of insubordination where matters of rank were involved. Had Henry not been so quarrelsome, petty, and jealous, his army career could have been more fruitful. But those above Henry were more likely to remember the flawed man who caused them so many headaches in camp, rather than his heroics on the battlefield.

Like all men of his time, Henry was a real person. He was a man of contradictions, able to keep an enslaved man by his side while fighting for independence. He could shake off physical wounds, but wounds to his pride were unforgettable and unforgivable. He was capable of good and bad, sometimes at the same time. It bears repeating that Henry was a real person. He was not a man to be celebrated as a paragon of virtue nor can the good that he did be completely dismissed either.

In the following pages, the story of the most formative years of his life will be laid bare. Heroics and juvenilities lain side by side. People are forever malleable both in life and death. In life, lessons learned or not learned can take people down very different paths. In death, the elements of one's life that are remembered shape the perception of that person—but as facts emerge and myths are disproven, the memory of that person can change. That is humanity. That is real life.

Here is the story of Henry's Revolution, it's successes and failures, its wins and losses.

Chapter One

The War Begins

THE FIRST RECORD of Henry Beekman Livingston being involved in the Revolution comes on June 6, 1775. He wrote to the New York State Congress to acknowledge receiving his commission as a captain in the army that New York was creating. The colonies were in full revolt following the attack on Lexington and Concord. The Battle of Bunker Hill was just days away. He was disappointed that his rank was lower than he had held in the British colonial militia. So far, he had also recruited ten men in Rhinebeck who needed arms and clothes (H. B. Livingston 1775).

This first letter from Henry shows a glimpse of the problematic man he could be when he did not have enough to do. His soon to be constant complaint, that his rank was not high enough, was on full display for the first time. He would never be satisfied with the rank he held and always reached for the next step. His complaint does give a clue that he held at least the rank of major in the colonial militia. His letters show that complaints about his rank filled his mind as equally as thoughts of his men did.

Henry Beekman Livingston has become nearly synonymous with the Revolutionary War in Rhinebeck. A historic marker indicates the ground where he drilled his men in front of what was then the Brinkerhoff Tavern, which is still in business as the Beekman Arms as of this writing. Next door at the Rhinebeck post office, a mural depicts Henry in his finest clothes plowing the ground, memorializing a local story that Henry did just that to insult King George III and make clear where he stood in the lead-up to the Revolution. By farming in what would have been considered his court clothes, had he ever been presented to the king, Henry was showing that he thought as much of the king as the dirt that he worked.

Henry continued to recruit during the summer months as the war continued elsewhere. The Battle of Bunker Hill came and went. On June 17, 1775, on a hill outside of the city of Boston, American militia men faced off against red-coated British soldiers. On what would prove a very bloody day, the British would end up holding the field at the cost of a tremendous amount of life. Yet the militia men could hold their heads high, knowing that in many cases they had fought until they ran out of ammunition and that the British had paid dearly for every inch of ground they had taken.

Still, Henry had nothing to do but train and recruit. Some of the men found other ways to entertain themselves about town, and at least one came down with a venereal disease after joining the Rhinebeck company. Henry had recruited at least seventy-two men, but he had no idea what to do with them (H. B. Livingston 1775).

Communication was so poor at the time that Henry had no idea what regiment he and his company belonged to nearly two months after he had received his commission (H. B. Livingston 1775). As it turned out, Livingston and his company belonged to the 4th New York Regiment under Colonel James Holmes, and their time for recruiting and training was soon over as they were assigned to the invasion of Canada. On August 17 the men received regimental coats and blankets from the state to prepare them to march into combat (New York Legislature 1842, 38).

This invasion was meant to bring the Canadian colonies over to the rebel side. The Canada that the colonists were referring to was Quebec and the parts of Canada further up the St. Lawrence River. The rest of Canada further down the St. Lawrence River and other areas like Nova Scotia, New Brunswick, and Newfoundland were considered too sparsely populated or too easily cut off by the British Navy to be of use in the Revolution. It was thought that a show of force in Canada would cause the largely francophone population of Quebec to throw off British governance and join their southern neighbors in the fight. Failing that, conquering the major settlements of Montreal and Quebec City would make it impossible for the British to invade the other colonies from the north by keeping reinforcements out of the St. Lawrence River.

This invasion was initially under the command of Major General Philip Schuyler, but repeated bouts of gout kept in him in New York, and command of the invasion devolved to the second in command, Brigadier General Richard Montgomery. Montgomery was Henry Beekman Livingston's brother-in-law, having married Henry's oldest sister Janet at Clermont in 1773. Montgomery was a former British officer who had fought in the French and Indian War. Following the war, he had resigned his commission and retired to a farm at Kingsbridge, New York to live the life of a gentleman farmer.

Retirement was not to be for Montgomery as the troubles between Britain and her colonies soon began. He was initially chosen as a representative to the New York convention. From there he was chosen, for his past military experience, as a brigadier general in the army. On his way through New York City to Boston to assume command of the army there, George Washington delivered Montgomery's brigadier general commission.

Montgomery had already begun the invasion by the time Henry received orders to join him. Henry marched his company to Fort George on Lake George, where he was forced to wait three days until boats were available to bring him and his men up the lake to Fort Ticonderoga. After consulting with the commanding officer there, Henry was told there were not enough boats to bring his entire company up Lake Champlain to join the army.

Rather than rest at the fort and wait for boats to become available, Henry took matters into his own hands. He obtained permission to leave his company at the fort while he caught a ride on one of the few boats going up the lake. He ordered his lieutenants to bring the men north as soon as the boats were available, but he would be going it alone until they arrived.

Henry joined the army encamped at Île aux Noix. Lieutenant Colonel Rudolphus Ritzema[1] of the 1st New York Regiment was ordered to take a party of troops to try to encircle the town of St. John's and cut it off from the rest of Canada. The army had laid siege to the town on September 17 and it was hoped that by completing the encirclement the town would surrender. Henry talked Ritzema into allowing him to accompany him as an aide-de-camp.

The party landed unopposed, and Colonel Ritzema assigned a flanking party to the woods. Montgomery stood off on the water with some boats to watch their advance. As they advanced, the officers suddenly found themselves almost completely bereft of troops. When Ritzema and Henry caught up to the fleeing men, they found that the men had panicked when the flanking party suddenly burst out of the woods to join the rest of the column. The main body had thought the returning flanking party was a body of native warriors coming to attack them.

After this inauspicious start, Ritzema and Livingston were able to get the army moving forward again. They had barely advanced one hundred yards when they came under attack from muskets ahead

[1] The Dutch-born Ritzema deserted the American army in the following year and served as a Lieutenant Colonel in the British Army, raising companies for the Royal American Reformers before being put on half pay.

of them and at least one cohorn mortar mounted in a boat on the water. The majority of the troops retreated again, except for the officers and about thirty men who found a breastwork in front of them protecting a party of fifteen made up of French colonists, English soldiers, and their native allies. After a brief fire-fight, one of the natives and one of the French colonists were killed, and the rest of the small party retreated.

Ritzema's command spent the night there and the next day and, despite haranguing by their officers, refused to advance one more step. General Montgomery was forced to take them off in boats and return them to Île aux Noix (Delafield 1889).

Thus, Henry's first time under fire was both a personal success and a professional failure. He had kept a cool head and not panicked as the musket balls flew, yet he and Ritzema were not able to keep their men under control to make any real headway against the enemy. The fact that this failure happened in full view of his brother-in-law and the commander of the army, General Montgomery, almost certainly stung Henry's pride.

The event was soon forgotten as other American forces did complete the encirclement of St. John's. The Fort surrendered on November 3, 1775. Montgomery quickly pushed his army on toward

Montreal, which fell almost without a shot fired on November 13, 1775.

Robert Livingston, Henry's brother and Montgomery's brother-in-law, congratulated Montgomery in a letter dated November 15, 1775. In it he mentioned that he had received word from Henry that he was considering resigning his commission, claiming he was "out of hopes of preferment." Robert speculated that he was "weary of serving under warrant officers whom he looks upon as his inferiors" (R. R. Livingston 1775). With no one to fight, Henry was becoming miserable in camp and was hoping for a promotion that would lift him above those he saw as his inferiors.

After the fall of Montreal, Montgomery called Henry to his headquarters and gave him dispatches to Congress telling of his success and orders to deliver them. Traditionally, in European style armies, the man who delivers news of a victory was rewarded by the monarch or other ruling power. In this case Montgomery may have been hoping for quick advancement for his brother-in-law by Congress, or he may have been trying to get him away from the army, where inaction was already beginning to wear on Henry's nerves. Montgomery had once written of Henry, "I would rather advise him to quit his present corps and get into a genteeler regiment should one be established" (Dangerfield 1960, 65).

On November 21 Henry had reached Albany with word of the fall of Montreal. He ran into Robert Treat Paine in the city, who soon wrote of the encounter to Henry's brother, Robert R. Livingston (Smith 1977, 369). Robert must have been extremely proud of both his brother-in-law Montgomery, for taking an important post like Montreal—and for Henry, being the bearer of the news knowing full well what that could mean for his career. Later in the month, Robert, who had at that point been sent on a fact-finding mission to Canada by Congress, wrote to his friend John Jay, who was still in Philadelphia, about Henry, "I have great satisfaction in the commendation he receives from all who have served with him." In the same letter, though, he warned Jay that Henry would need help in the more genteel company of Philadelphia. "If he is still with you I beg you take him by the hand, you will find amongst his roughness many good qualities" (Smith 1977, 398).

Henry was indeed still in Philadelphia, and he apparently did not much like Robert sending his close confidant Jay to look after him. Jay wrote in December that he had gone to Henry's lodgings with Henry's cousin Philip Livingston, to ask Henry to dinner. Finding that he was already engaged for dinner with James Duane, Jay invited himself along. Jay felt that from that day on Henry did his best to avoid him, writing to Robert: "I am not without my suspicion relative to his behavior which you will easily guess & shall induce him to explain to you." No evidence survives that Henry ever explained himself to his brother in regard to Jay, but perhaps he felt having Jay looking out for him was the same as having his big brother looking over his shoulder (Smith 1977, 495). While Henry welcomed his brother interceding on his behalf politically or using his family name for advancement, he did not feel the need for a babysitter.

Finally, on December 20, 1775 came the day Henry had been waiting for. Congress had decided on his reward for delivering the news of the fall of Montreal. It was ordered that he would receive "a handsome sword" and a promise that he would be promoted as soon as a position for him became available (Smith 1977, 500).

Henry must have been ecstatic. His advancement in the army was all but guaranteed. He thanked Congress profusely in a letter read before them on December 22, 1775. "Their present is amazing, genteel, and their promise very flattering to a young man who wishes to acquire a reputation." Henry would have delivered the remarks in person, but he had either just found out about his father's death or was using his father's death as an excuse not to appear before Congress: "These I would beg leave to present in person, did not my affection for my late father render me unfit to appear before them (E. B. Livingston 1998).

Henry's father, Judge Robert R. Livingston had died on December 9, 1775. As a relatively young man of only fifty-seven, the Judge's death came unexpectedly. He simply went to his bed and passed away either from a heart attack, stroke, or something similarly quick. The Judge's death came less than six months after his own father Robert's death, and mere weeks before Henry's maternal grandfather and namesake Colonel Henry Beekman would die on January 3, 1776. Amidst all of this death came the news that Richard Montgomery had been killed in the early hours of January 1, 1776 in a last-ditch assault on the city of Quebec. Having bottled up the entire Canadian garrison in the city—joined by another small army that had been led to Canada by Benedict Arnold through the wilds of what is now Maine, Montgomery planned one more attack on the city before his men's enlistments ran out. Quebec was divided into an upper and lower town. Arnold was severely wounded attacking the upper town, and

Montgomery was killed by a blast of grapeshot from a cannon attacking the lower town. The attack fell apart, and despite later reinforcements Quebec City never fell to the Americans.

Henry's brother, Robert, was quite shaken by all these deaths, but Henry seems to have born up. Robert spent several weeks at his home confined to bed. Henry, on the other hand, was intent to do his duty, especially when his promotion finally came through.

Chapter Two

The Battle for New York

THE BRITISH ARMY was forced to abandon the city of Boston on March 17, 1776. Up to that point Boston had been the center of the war, with the British army bottled up in the city by what had become to be known as the Continental Army after a Congressional resolution on June 14, 1775. The British could not sortie out in force as illness and food shortages had begun to take hold, while the Continentals were unwilling to storm and possibly destroy the city. They were at a stalemate until Henry Knox showed up with dozens of cannons transported from Fort Ticonderoga to Boston. It was one of the greatest feats of logistics and perseverance of the war. Knox brought the heavy artillery—which had been captured the previous summer by Benedict Arnold, Ethan Allen, and the Green Mountain Boys—more than three hundred miles from Fort Ticonderoga to Boston, starting from the Fort on December 6, 1775 and arriving at Boston on January 27, 1776. Once the cannons were placed on Dorchester Heights above Boston on March 4, the British packed up what they could and left the city by ship, headed for Nova Scotia.

It was generally understood that this was not the end of the war. The British would be back, but the question was, where? George Washington gambled that the British would attack New York City, so he moved the bulk of his army there and began to fortify. In addition to fortifying the city, fortifications were established further up the Hudson River in the Hudson Highlands to prevent incursions up the river by the British Navy. It was feared that they could surround the island of Manhattan or even strike further up the river into the Hudson Valley.

Henry was promoted to Lieutenant Colonel of the 2nd New York Regiment in March 1776 under Colonel James Clinton. His first orders did not come until May 4 though, when George Washington ordered him to take command of four companies of the 2nd New York stationed at Fort Montgomery and Fort Constitution in the Hudson Highlands. He was further ordered to repair there, take command of the forts, and finish the fortifications (Washington May 4, 1776). The forts were strategically located on a bend in the river which, it was hoped, British ships would have trouble navigating, giving the forts time to rain cannon balls down on the ships, therefore preventing the British from getting any further up the river.

During his time at the Highland forts, Livingston came to believe the biggest impediment to successfully completing his orders was not the British but his own side. His first and biggest challenge was Colonel Isaac Nicoll of the Orange County Militia. Colonel Nicoll had been in command of the forts when they were manned by the militia, but their enlistments had expired. When a Continental officer had been sent to relieve him, Nicoll should have gone home. Initially, he left after Henry had been there for five days but soon returned and stayed until June 8, one day shy of a full month after Henry arrived to take command (H. B. Livingston to Washington June 11–14, 1776).

General William Alexander, Lord Stirling, commended Henry in a letter to George Washington for not instigating a dispute with Colonel Nicoll during their shared time there. Instead of fighting, Henry simply went about his business of constructing the forts as well as he could without Nicoll's interference (Stirling 1776). This is most impressive for a man that historian George Dangerfield called "brave as a lion but arrogant, rough and almost pathologically quarrelsome..." (Dangerfield 1960, 64–65). Despite not fighting with Nicoll over command of the forts, Henry was sure to mention Nicoll's continued, unwanted presence in several letters to George Washington and John McKesson.

Henry had arrived at the forts on May 9, 1776 and had been immediately taken aback by their poor condition. They still lacked basic buildings such as infirmaries and enough barracks to house all the men. The soldiers of the garrison were in rough shape as well. They were required to work nine hours a day building fortifications but received fresh food only once in a month. Some men were beginning to show signs of scurvy from a lack of fresh vegetables (H. B. Livingston to Washington May 14, 1776). Henry also noted that Fort Constitution was dominated by a higher point on the Hudson called West Point. If cannons were placed on the point, they could fire directly into Fort Constitution. He suggested fortifying that location as well (H. B. Livingston to Washington June 11–14, 1776).

During his time in command in the Hudson Valley, Henry received shipments of arms meant to help the defenders of the forts as well as a shipment of loyalist prisoners to be used as laborers. Henry absolutely refused to use the prisoners as labor, calling it "tyrannical." The weapons he found almost worthless as well, including a shipment of fifty-eight stands of arms that came in from Dutchess County that were found to be mostly inoperative (H. B. Livingston to Washington May 21, 1776). Even more ridiculous, Livingston Manor sent him several seven-foot-long fowling pieces designed for shooting water fowl, but their large size and slow loading time made them nearly useless on the battlefield. Henry had to get creative with the authority and resources he had. He soon found four soldiers who had previous experience with weapons to act as armorers and gunsmiths. Instead of building fortifications, they were given the job of making the weapons on hand as ready for use as possible (H. B. Livingston to Washington June 11–14, 1776).

On June 14 Henry was ordered to be replaced at the forts by Colonel James Clinton, Commander of the 2nd New York Regiment (Washington June 14, 1776). Henry was sent to Long Island to take command of four companies of the 2nd New York Regiment that were stationed there. His troops would be the eastern-most on Long Island, serving as sentinels, should the British try to invade Long Island from there.

In July 1776 Henry sent a letter to George Washington detailing his position on the island shortly after the British fleet began to arrive in New York Harbor. The British fleet that arrived at New York represented the largest seaborne force ever assembled. Thirty-four thousand soldiers and sailors floated in the harbor while the Americans waited with bated breath to see where they would come ashore. Henry had two field pieces but no ammunition or tools to make them serviceable. He had spread his companies to Montauk Point, Shelter Island, and Oyster Pond Point. The company at Montauk Point was guarding about 1,600 cattle, 500 horses, and 10,000 sheep—valuable supplies the British would want if they landed on the island. The local Committee of Safety had provided Henry with five whale boats with which he could move men or even some of the animals, should the need arise (H. B. Livington July 1776). Henry's defenses were considered good enough that the Convention of New York wrote to the Committees of East and South Hampton that they should not worry about their stock as long as boats were provided in the case of danger (Convention of New York 1776).

On July 20, 1776, Nathaniel Woodhull requested that George Washington leave Henry and his men on the Eastern tip of the island and not have them join the main army. He claimed that "the Inhabitants would totally abandon the Country should those

Troops be drawn off" (Woodhull 1776). Despite the fact that Woodhull was later killed by loyalist troops, according to historian W. H. W. Sabine, he may have had a more sinister reason for trying to keep Livingston on the Eastern tip of the island and away from the main army. As evidence of Woodhull's duplicity, Sabine posits that Woodhull had offered to give up Suffolk County to the British and shows that Woodhull arrested no Tories, burned no mills, and never linked up with Henry (Sabine 1954, 103, 203). Once again, Henry learned that his opponents were not always men in red coats.

Henry wrote to his brother Robert to lament his position on August 21, 1776. "I much fear that the distance I am removed to, instead of Encouraging the affection of those I am connected to, has diminished them." His main fear was not that he was isolated on the east end of Long Island though, but that he would be superseded for command of the 2nd New York Regiment when Colonel Clinton was promoted to brigadier general. If that were to happen, Henry would be forced to resign and settle on a farm to "cultivate that portion heaven has assigned me." Of course, Henry did not resign his commission; there was a battle coming.

On August 22, 1776 the British began landing on Long Island. Within two days they had landed

20,000 men and began to push the main army on the island to the western end. On August 27 the two armies clashed in the Battle of Long Island. Starting in the early hours of the day, the British pressed the Americans hard. George Washington arrived on the Island in the early morning to take direct control of the army. After a full day of fighting and a few valiant stands by certain American units, the remnants of the army retreated to fortifications on Brooklyn Heights. General William Howe, leading the British army, began to prepare to lay siege to the works on the Heights. After a day in these positions Washington decided to retreat from Long Island and take what was left of his army to Manhattan. During the night of August 29–30, 1776, the Americans were rowed by John Glover's regiment of Marble Head fishermen to Manhattan. The Americans had abandoned Long Island.

Except for Henry.

Henry and his 200 men of the 2nd New York Regiment soon realized they were the only American force left on Long Island. The situation was dire. Henry was behind enemy lines, outnumbered by more than one hundred to one, and guarding a cache of supplies the British desperately needed. Henry wrote to Washington from Sag Harbor on August 30 (1776) that "The Publick Spirit of this

Country has reduced its Militia to nothing". The locals were completely demoralized and the people, the militia, were looking after themselves, their families, and their possessions. Henry was without support but intended to make the best showing he could. He wrote to Governor Johnathan Trumbull of Connecticut, who later forwarded the letter to Washington. He feared his detachment was in danger but would endeavor "to keep our reputations clear and unsullied, and, with our feeble force, to endeavor to distress our enemies all in our power" (H. B. Livingston August 30, 1776). The lion in Henry was beginning to show.

With the British supplying themselves with resources taken from their rear on Long Island, Henry Beekman Livingston set out to the west to harass their foraging parties (H. B. Livingston to Washington August 31, 1776). This was the first action in Henry's personal campaign against the British on Long Island. Despite the fact that Washington had essentially abandoned him to his fate, writing, "it is not in my power to give you any other instructions for your Conduct than that you pursue every step which shall appear to you necessary & judicious for annoying and harassing the Enemy" (Washington September 4, 1776).

Henry stayed on Long Island until September

4 (Washington September 4, 1776). He had hoped to continue on the island, even making plans for the next night for he and his men to be "unexpected guests at a meeting in Southold where Col. Phineas Fanning was set to issue an oath of allegiance to the crown to the people of the town" (H. B. Livingston to Trumbull September 4, 1776). Henry realized, though, that his position was untenable and retreated from Long Island to the relative safety of Connecticut, but he remained determined to continue his private war on the British and loyalists on the island.

On September 7, 1776 Henry and his detachment crossed Long Island Sound to raid the island. He captured 307 small arms and brought off several refugees: men, women, and children with anti-British leanings who were trapped on the island (H. B. Livingston September 7, 1776). On September 10 Henry was back in Saybrook, Connecticut, writing to Governor Trumbull about capturing Colonel Abram Gardiner, who had been "soliciting" oaths of allegiance to the King at gunpoint. To Washington he wrote that his detachment had grown to more than 400 men with the addition of local militia men, and he had taken an additional 236 small arms and 6 cannons in addition to: five and a half quarter-casks of gunpowder, two and a half boxes of musket balls,

190 cartridge boxes, 160 powder horns, and 153 bayonets (H. B. Livingston to Washington September 11, 1776). These arms and accoutrements would be used to equip more American troops in the fight against the British.

On September 24 Henry informed George Washington of his most recent excursion on Long Island. The raid had captured 3,129 sheep and 400 cows. Henry's men had also tried to capture Richard Miller, who was attempting to raise a loyalist company on the eastern end of the island. Miller tried to run when the Americans appeared and was shot and killed by his pursuers.

During this raid on Long Island Henry obtained a bit of intelligence that he was quite proud of. General Oliver Delancey, commander of loyalist forces, had placed a £500 price on his head. Someone, even if it was the enemy, was noticing the fighting that Henry was doing and the success he was having. Perhaps his own side would soon take notice of him too.

Henry boasted that with a few more men he could take back Jamaica if not push the British off the island altogether as the main army had crossed the river (H. B. Livingston to Washington September 24, 1776). He was never given the chance though.

He also wrote to his brother Robert the same day. He bragged about the sheep and cattle he had brought off Long Island and the price on his head. He went into a little more detail about Richard Miller, claiming that he had already recruited forty men for his company and that he would have been a formidable enemy "if he had not been cut short." In the same letter he complained that he was almost out of money himself but that if a debt Walter Livingston owed him could be collected, he would be all right. He also suggested his brothers Robert and John consider buying paper money on Long Island where a dollar bill could be purchased for a pence hard money. The exchange rate could have made them a tidy sum of money. It is unlikely that either brother acted on Henry's suggestion, as traveling to Long Island, particularly for Robert, a drafter of the Declaration of Independence, would have been foolhardy and reckless (H. B. Livingston to R. Livingston September 24,1776).

Intelligence provided to Henry by Governor Jonathan Trumbull of Connecticut often saved Henry a great deal of pain on Long Island. For instance, on October 13 Trumbull wrote to Henry that the "infamous" Major Robert Rogers was on Long Island raising troops. Trumbull feared an attack on Norwalk, Connecticut where a great deal of Continental stores was being kept. He also warned Henry that Rogers was "a famous scouter, or woods-hunter, skilled in waylaying, ambuscade and sudden attacks." In short, Henry should watch out for ambush on his next visit to the island (Trumbull 1776).

Henry made one more large-scale raid on the island on October 28. In addition to whale boats that had been Henry's typical mode of transportation across the sound to that point, Henry brought a sloop named *The Spy*, which was piloted by Caleb Brewster. The raid was supposed to consist of Henry's men and a detachment of soldiers from Rhode Island. Colonel Richmond of Rhode Island refused to embark most of his troops, which meant that, rather than a large-scale attack, this would be another raid. On the way across the sound *The Spy* grounded, but Henry continued in a whale boat. The raid captured two sloops and a great deal of arms and accoutrements (New York Legislature 1842, 2:364–365).

During the excursion to Long Island, Henry's men and the few Rhode Island men he had with him attacked the headquarters of a Captain Smith's company of Oliver Delancey's brigade. The loyalists were waiting for them and opened fire, killing one of the men from Rhode Island and wounding another. Henry's force returned fire, killing seven loyalists and wounding two. The rest, including Captain Smith, surrendered to Henry. This victory inspired

Henry to further action. He wanted to attack and break up Delancey's entire brigade, but the officers of Rhode Island refused to help with this engagement, and Henry was forced to retreat. In addition to the two sloops named *Princess Mary* and *Lily* that were loaded with firewood intended for New York City, a schooner was captured that would be fitted out as a privateer (H. B. Livingston to R. Livingston September 1776; Roe 1904, 16).

Caleb Brewster would stay on with Livingston and become an ensign in the 4th New York Regiment until he was promoted into an artillery regiment in November 1777 (Public Papers of George Clinton 1900, vol.2). Brewster went on to become part of the Culper Spy Ring, ferrying messages from Long Island across the Long Island Sound to Connecticut, where they could be delivered to George Washington.

Perhaps Henry's most important work during his stint raiding Long Island was rescuing refugees from the British occupation of the island. He had taken the sloop *Dove* into the service specifically for the rescue mission. From September 5 until October 14 the sloop carried refugees, their possessions, and as much livestock as possible across Long Island Sound to Connecticut (Mather 2010, 800). Still, there were more refugees than Henry could handle. On September 15 he wrote that the wharves of

Sag Harbor were covered with "our friends," men and their families who had elected to perish rather than fight against the Americans (H. B. Livingston to Trumbull September 15, 1776). Sometimes, the refugees were the families of men Henry had recruited for his regiment. On the September 24 raid across the sound, Captain Daniel Roe of the 2nd New York Regiment brought off his family, their goods, and a number of other people (Roe 1904, 15). Refugees fled Long Island as the British stole their livestock and crops for their own use. Those who stayed starved and were accosted by the rampaging Ministerial army.

Chapter Three

Back to The Hudson Valley

By the end of November Henry's time attacking Long Island was at an end. He was promoted to full colonel and given command of the 4th New York Regiment. He was stationed in the lower Hudson Valley under the command of General Alexander McDougall (H. B. Livingston to New York Committee of Arrangement 1776).

From the very beginning of their relationship, McDougall and Henry spent more time fighting each other than they did the British. McDougall was an immigrant who had worked his way up from milk-delivery boy to become a privateer during the French and Indian War. After the war, McDougall went on to become a merchant in New York but was too low-born to be accepted by high-born families, such as the Livingstons, into New York society. As his brother had observed in 1775, Henry could not bear to serve under officers he considered his inferiors. It was Henry's belief that he was better than McDougall both in social standing and military ability that led to much of their conflict. For Henry it was all right to invest in privateers but not to associate with them (H. B. Livingston, Account Book n.d.).

Early in his colonelcy Henry was focused internally on the regiment. The regiment was short of men, so officers were sent out to recruit. The regiment also lacked a lieutenant colonel, so Henry requested Lieutenant Colonel Pierre Regnier. Regnier was a Frenchman who had joined the American army in 1775 and was promoted to lieutenant colonel in 1776, which indicates that some thought he showed promise as an officer (*Louisiana Gazette* 1810). A few days after Henry's request, John Jay, a close friend of Henry's brother Robert, made his own recommendation to Washington that Regnier be made Lieutenant Colonel of the 4th New York Regiment (Jay 1777). The same day John Jay made his recommendation, Washington wrote back to Henry to say that he would recommend Regnier to the New York Committee to fill the role. A few days later it was done. Regnier was officially Lieutenant Colonel of the 4th New York Regiment.

This letter from Washington also quashed the final hope that Henry had of returning to Long

Island as a conquering hero. He wrote "I would advise the Expedition you had in view be laid aside. I do not think it improbable that your services may be wanted elsewhere and upon some more interesting occasion" (Washington to H. B. Livingston February 20, 1777). To Washington, Long Island was lost and he would not be sending any of his limited number of troops to try to retake it.

Henry had trouble recruiting for his regiment in the Hudson Valley. He felt that the bounties offered in New England and for short term enlistments in the militia were preferable to what he could offer (H. B. Livingston to Washington March 7, 1777). It probably did not help that in the five months Henry had commanded the regiment, his men had not been paid. If word of that spread, why would anyone want to join his regiment (H. B. Livingston to Washington March 12, 1777)? On the other hand, Henry was able to retain some of the men he had worked with on Long Island, including several of his officers who had joined him in his fight on Long Island.

By the March 12, McDougall had assembled his troops, including Henry's regiment, at Peekskill. They were there to guard stores and munitions for the army. It was also the site where the relationship between Henry and McDougall reached its peak of acrimony.

On Sunday, March 23, the British sailed four transports up the river under the cover of a frigate to attack Peekskill. Colonel Ann Hawkes Hay reported from across the river on the day of the attack that he saw the troops land and a large fire that consumed the upper barracks, "if not the whole town of Peekskill, it is said done by our own people" (Hay 1777).

Having been at Peekskill, Henry had a slightly different account. At the landing of the British troops, he was ordered by McDougall to retreat while burning the military buildings and stores. He first stopped 400 yards beyond the town and waited for more orders. When they came, they called for him to retreat farther away from the town. On Monday, March 24, a British scouting party was turned back by the 3rd New York Regiment, but on Tuesday the British troops were allowed to leave without any attempt at an attack while they were vulnerable as they reboarded their ships (H. B. Livingston to Washington March 29, 1777).

McDougall did not report the losses to Washington until March 29. He admitted to having advance notice of the attack but doing nothing. The fleet that arrived had grown from that which Hay had seen. McDougall reported the presence of a frigate, three gallies, two ships, two brigs, four transports, and a variety of smaller craft. Before the troops had even set foot on land, McDougall ordered the destruction of the supplies he was supposed to guard. This included arms and ammunition for 500 men, 100 hogsheads of rum and sugar, 60 boxes of soap and candles, 600 barrels of flour and 30 tons of iron. All this was destroyed, in addition to several buildings, including his men's barracks and a mill. McDougall would go on to claim that the British had suffered at least thirteen casualties during skirmishing, and he had only suffered one man killed (McDougall 1777).

Henry Beekman Livingston called the events at Peekskill "a damn scandalous retreat" (E. B. Livingston 1998, 242–243). He thought that McDougall was a coward (H. B. Livingston to R. Livingston June 30, 1777). Needless to say, his relationship with McDougall did not improve in the months that followed. On May 19,1777 he asked to be removed from McDougall's command saying, "I am convinced my stay here will be productive of the worst consequences to my reputation" (H. B. Livingston to Washington May 19, 1777). Washington responded that Henry should lodge a complaint with General Israel Putnam, who was McDougall's immediate superior. A court of Inquiry could be convened and the dispute between the two would be resolved (Washington June 1, 1777).

This did not happen, and their relationship continued to deteriorate. By the time General Putnam arrived at Peekskill, McDougall had placed Livingston under arrest and was waiting for more officers to arrive so he could convene a general court martial. McDougall was charging Henry with traducing the character of General McDougall in ordering the retreat at Peekskill, for neglecting to bring his regiment in a timely manner, and for using language abusive to McDougall, and conduct unbecoming an officer and a gentleman. Henry was also suspected of circulating a letter that Putnam called "mutiny." Henry was never proven to be the author. At his court martial, Henry was found guilty of breach of respect but not to the extent that it was conduct unbecoming an officer and a gentleman. His sentence was to sustain a rebuke in the next day's orders (Putnam to Washington June 10, 1777).

That should have been the end of it, but Henry continued to be his quarrelsome self while cooped up in camp. He challenged McDougall to a duel, which McDougall declined. He asked Putnam to arrest McDougall, which Putnam refused. McDougall wanted to arrest Henry again. At this point Putnam stepped in and negotiated a cease-fire between the two men (Putnam to Washington June 9, 1777). McDougall claimed that he did not want to see

Henry removed from the army but stated, not without a note of jealousy, that Henry had unto that point always had an independent command and did not know how to function in the larger army (Putnam to Washington June 10, 1777).

Still stinging from the rebuke he received at his court martial, Henry was ordered to Morrisania, the manor of Gouverneur Morris's family, to catch a body of British reported to be there. Putnam also sent Colonel Philip Van Cortlandt and gave Van Cortlandt command of the expedition, reasoning that he was more familiar with the terrain. Henry immediately returned to Putnam's headquarters, insulted once again, as he believed he outranked Van Cortlandt, according to a commission from Congress. Van Cortlandt believed he was the superior officer because of his commission from New York State (Putnam to Washington June 9, 1777). These disputes were not uncommon among many officers in the Continental Army, but coming on the heels of his dispute with McDougall, it did not make Henry look particularly good in the eyes of Putnam.

When a request came for troops to reinforce the Northern Army against the invasion by General John Burgoyne, Henry quickly found himself heading north, away from McDougall and back toward battle.

The British strategy in 1777 consisted of three

forces who would march simultaneously, crush the American Northern Department militia units between them, then conquer Albany, which would leave them in control of the entire Hudson River. They also hoped that this motion would draw out George Washington for a pitched battle, where they could defeat his army and be done with him as well. The British thought this strategy would equate to cutting the head off a snake, believing that without New England, the Revolution would wither and die.

General John Burgoyne would lead an army south out of Canada and down the Champlain and Hudson valleys to Albany. General Barry St. Leger would lead an army out of Canada to the west and march along the Mohawk Valley toward Albany. General William Howe would bring his army out of New York City and march north along the Hudson River on his way to Albany.

The plan met with some early success. General Burgoyne was able to take Fort Ticonderoga and made his way, slowly, south. St. Leger was laying siege to Fort Stanwix in the west with the hope that it would fall any day. General Howe chose not to follow the plan.

Howe had decided, with governmental permission but without telling Burgoyne, to attack Philadelphia. In traditional European warfare, capturing your enemy's capital was tantamount to victory. He managed to draw Washington into battle at the Battle of Brandywine and take Philadelphia. Soon after, at the Battle of Germantown Washington suffered another defeat and realized he could not take back the city.

Howe left General Henry Clinton in command of New York City. At first Clinton did not think he would be able to do anything to help with the three-pronged attack on the river, but thanks to some well-timed reinforcements, he was able to muster together a force of a few thousand men, consisting of British regulars, Hessian mercenaries, and loyalists to lead up the river. They were not going to be of assistance in defeating any army, but they could perhaps provide a distraction that would assist Burgoyne's or St. Leger's armies.

The Northern Department of the Continental Army had moved into place near Saratoga. Their position would prevent Burgoyne from continuing down the Hudson River without a conflict. Once in camp near Saratoga, the 4th New York Regiment was assigned to General Enoch Poor‘s brigade as part of the division under the command of General Benedict Arnold. Henry and the 4th New York were only in camp one day when they were sent to the west to join Arnold's movement to relieve the siege of Fort Stanwix. They returned to camp on August

29 without a fight, after General Barry St. Leger had given up his siege and had begun a retreat to Canada, thanks to a clever ploy by Arnold (Luzander 2008, 187). Arnold sent a man ahead of his army to warn St. Leger's native allies that he was coming. Arnold's reputation was enough to cause the natives to desert St. Leger. Without the native warriors, St. Leger did not have the men to continue the siege and was forced to lead what was left of his army back toward Canada.

On September 19 Arnold faced off against the British Army at the Battle of Freeman's Farm, also known as the first Battle of Saratoga. Early that morning the British moved on the American position. American commanding officer Horatio Gates was happy to sit back and accept the frontal assault, but Arnold feared a flanking maneuver and was allowed to take a small group of men to counter the threat. The attack did come on the flank and early in the afternoon the 4th New York Regiment was among the regiments sent to reinforce the line there. The battle raged back and forth across farm fields for more than two hours as the sides took turns charging each other. The Americans would capture the British cannon only to be pushed back again. As darkness set in, the British sent in more reinforcements, and the Americans retreated back to the defenses they had prepared. The British held the field but had lost nearly 600 men. The Americans had lost 300. The 4th New York was in the thick of the fighting that day, and Henry would later receive Benedict Arnold's compliments for his actions during the battle (Luzander 2008, 384).

Like Arnold, Henry wanted to attack the British the next day. Henry assumed the idea of attacking again was rejected by Gates simply because it was presented by Arnold. Arnold and Gates had a contentious relationship brought on in part by their opposing views on fighting. Arnold liked to take the fight to the enemy while Gates preferred to dig in and fight from behind fortifications. The American army began digging in and allowing the British army to do the same (H. B. Livingston to R. Livingston October 4,1777).

In the interim between battles, relations between Arnold and Gates continued to break down. Gates had replaced General Philip Schuyler before the Battle of Freeman's Farm as overall commander of the Northern Department. Schuyler was a wealthy landlord before the war who had achieved his military rank because of his social rank. Gates was a former British officer who had chosen to fight for the Americans. Like many other former European officers, he felt that he deserved higher rank in the army than his colonial counterparts. Surprisingly, Henry had no issue with the replacement despite seeing Schuyler as a rare social equal in the army. Perhaps he still remembered the convenient case of gout that led Schuyler to give command of the invasion of Canada to Richard Montgomery, which ultimately led to Montgomery's death. As things between Gates and Arnold became more acrimonious, Arnold decided to leave camp. Henry was among the colonels of General Poor's brigade who signed an appeal for General Arnold to remain (Luzander 2008, 211, 268).

Weeks later, on October 7, at the Battle of Bemis Heights, the 4th New York Regiment once again found itself in the heat of battle. The British had set out in what they called a recognizance in force, which was meant to scout the American lines and harvest wheat from a field to supplement their rapidly vanishing provisions. They were met by General Learned's and General Poor's brigades. The 4th New York Regiment found itself holding the right end of the American line in the wheat field where the battle was being fought. Henry's lion began to roar.

The two sides had fought to a near standstill when the sudden appearance of a large contingent of the

Albany County militia, nearly 1,200 men, including the Livingston Manor militia, appeared on the field. The British spirit was broken and so was their line.

When the British broke, they retreated to two redoubts in the British line, one commanded by Lord Balcarres and the other by the Hessian Heinrich von Breymann. Poor's men, including the 4th New York, attacked Balcarres's redoubt and were rebuffed (Dangerfield 1960, 103,467). When Benedict Arnold decided to attack von Breymann's redoubt, Henry and the 4th New York Regiment were the first Americans to follow him. Henry wrote. "In the last engagement my regiment was the first that entered the enemies lines, and I believe I can safely affirm that I was the first man in there next to Genl Arnold who was on Horse Back." (H. B. Livingston to R. Livingston October 14, 1777). In addition to being indicative of Henry's bravery in battle, this statement also seems to indicate that Henry was not riding his horse for some reason. The reason he was not on horseback was most likely because his enslaved servant Jack was charged with changing his horse for his mare back in Rhinebeck.

Throughout the war Henry was accompanied by a slave named Jack. Jack's duties would have included packing and unpacking Henry's possessions at different camps, washing and brushing Henry's clothes, taking care of Henry's horse, and anything else Henry needed done. In short, Jack was charged with doing everything that Henry did not want to do or could not do for himself. After the Second Battle of Saratoga, Jack was sent from the camp near Stillwater to deliver a letter to Robert Livingston. He was also charged with switching Henry's horse for his mare. The horse may have been lame or unusable in battle. This could explain why Henry was on foot during the attack on the redoubt. Powius, possibly another of Henry's enslaved people, was to take care of the horse (H. B. Livingston to R. Livingston October 10,1777). The fact that Jack could make this trip on his own indicates a significant amount of trust placed in the enslaved man. Jack could have ridden the horse to freedom and lost himself in the chaos created by the war, but instead he did what was asked of him and returned to Henry's side and would be there for more of the suffering Henry would endure during the war.

While recovering from a leg wound received while attacking the redoubt, Arnold took the time to commend Henry for his bravery on October 7 (Dangerfield 1960, 101, 128). Robert Livingston wrote to George Washington in December of 1777 to remind him that Henry had distinguished himself at both battles and been commended by General

Arnold. Then he asked that Henry be offered the command of a partisan corps (R. Livingston to George Washington December 8, 1777).

Burgoyne surrendered his army on October 17, 1777. Henry was there to witness the surrender. Following the battles, General Horatio Gates sent Henry on a mission that required tact, finesse, and diplomacy. He would have to put the lion and the quarrel away.

While the battles of Saratoga raged, General Henry Clinton, the British commanding officer in New York City, set out north on the Hudson River. He took the Highland Forts that Henry had worked to build: Fort Montgomery, Fort Clinton, and Fort Constitution. He pulled the large chain the Americans had blocking the river out of the water. Then he then sent a force further north under the command of a subordinate named John Vaughn to determine if there was anything that could be done to relieve Burgoyne. That force burned the city of Kingston to the ground and then moved slightly further north on the river to burn down Clermont, Henry's childhood home, and all its outbuildings on October 18, 1777, the day after Burgoyne's army in the North had surrendered.

Henry was ordered to go to Fort Montgomery,

where it was expected he would find General Clinton. However, upon hearing that Burgoyne had surrendered, Clinton had abandoned the forts and retreated to New York City. Henry chose to exceed his orders and continue south in pursuit of Clinton. Keeping in mind that Henry was alone on this mission, it seemed that the lion had not yet completely settled down. Henry made it all the way to Kingsbridge, where he was picked up by the British frigate *Mercury*, commanded by Captain James Montagu who came from a famous family of British sailors. Henry was allowed to write one letter to General Clinton while he was aboard the frigate (H. B. Livingston to Governor George Clinton 1777).

In part, the letter read; "Helpless widows and children are left exposed to all the inclemecies [*sic*] of the approaching winter. This conduct sufficiently evinces your despair of ever conquering the Country. The Fortune of War has placed in our Power an Officer of Equal Rank to that you hold and whose prospects of success were greater than any you now can flatter yourself with. You Sir may not always be exempted from the Calamities of War. Accident or injuries may one Day subject you to the same fate. Should your further Conduct be delineated by such Horrid Barbarity. Our utmost Efforts may prove ineffectual to preserve you from the resentment of a justly incensed people" (H. B. Livingston to General Henry Clinton 1777).

Henry waited aboard the *Mercury* for several days but did not receive an answer from Clinton. When Montagu would not consent to let him send another letter, Henry departed, having "met with very Indifferent Treatment on Board" (H. B. Livingston to Governor George Clinton 1777).

Henry returned to his regiment a few days after writing to George Clinton about his experience on board the *Mercury*. Poor's brigade with the 4th New York still attached was transferred from the Northern Department to the main Continental Army under the command of General George Washington. They had marched through Henry's old stomping grounds of Peekskill, where Poor and Israel Putnam met. Poor was hesitant to give up the 4th New York and Putnam was absolutely dead set against having the 4th back under his command. So, the 4th officially became part of the main army (Hamilton 1777). Henry finally got something he had wished for most of the war, to be under the command of a man he considered worthy of leading him, George Washington. Washington and his army were about to settle into the most transformative winter an American army had ever experienced.

Chapter Four

Valley Forge

DURING THE LONG march from Saratoga to Pennsylvania, Henry and his men took comfort in the fact that they would be wintering comfortably in Philadelphia. They were shocked and discouraged to find the British in their expected winter quarters. As Henry put it, "they still occupy our proposed quarters without interruption and are as like to do so this winter." The army would have to find somewhere else to winter over (H. B. Livingston to R. Livingston November 30, 1777).

The army marched into Valley Forge on December 19, 1777. The soldiers of the Northern Department, like Henry's 4th New York Regiment had met with tremendous success at Saratoga, forcing the surrender of a large British army. The main army under General George Washington had not been so lucky. They had suffered defeat at the Battle of Brandywine on September 11, 1777, where after nearly eleven hours of fighting, both the left and right flanks of the American army collapsed, leading to a mass retreat. This allowed General William Howe and the British Army to seize Philadelphia on September 26, 1777. The Battle of Germantown on October 4, 1777 saw a dense fog throw an American attack on the British into chaos. American fired on American, direction was lost, and the American army retreated. Washington came no closer to seizing back Philadelphia. The morale of Washington's army that marched into the winter camp was at a low ebb.

Soon Livingston's men were feeling as bad as the rest of the army. Supplies ran short almost immediately. On December 24 Henry wrote to his brother Robert in the hope that Robert could use his position and standing in the New York State government to arrange for more supplies for his troops. There was no liquor of any kind to be had, no sugar or vegetables. He wrote that his men were nearly naked and starving. Only eighteen of the hundreds of men assigned to his regiment could report for duty fully dressed and fully armed. They were attempting to build huts to shelter themselves from the winter weather "without nails or tools so that I suppose we may render ourselves very comfortable by the time winter is over." On top of everything else, his men were becoming lousy with bugs, a fate that he himself shared. Jack had left four of his spare shirts behind somewhere and the rest were lost as his trunk of clothes was misplaced somewhere between Albany and Valley Forge. Henry believed the ship the trunk was on was either sunk or taken by the enemy (H. B. Livingston to R. Livingston December 24, 1777). In short Henry did not have a clean shirt to his name and no way to acquire one.

The next day, Christmas, Henry wrote to Governor George Clinton of New York to appeal for more supplies for his men. He pleaded that his men were "Wholly destitute of clothing" and that the men and officers were "perishing in the field." He then appealed to Clinton's New York State pride, telling him that troops from other states were receiving supplies from their home states. At this point, even though their own regiments were part of the Continental Army, the states were still supposed to be supplying them. He also suggested that without supplies the men would begin deserting and the regiment would be forced to disband, making New York look bad in the eyes of all the other states. Henry concluded the letter by saying that he hoped Clinton could do something for his men so "that the troops of the state of New York will no longer be ashamed to appear in the field with those of other states" (Clinton 1900, 2:605–606).

The winter at Valley Forge was certainly not easy on the army, but their suffering has been exaggerated over time. According to Valley Forge National Historical Park, food supplies began to arrive in January 1778, and most of the men were fully clothed by March. Much has been made of the harsh weather that winter, when in fact the winter was relatively mild. Although it did snow, and freezes were frequent at night, the days were often warm enough to thaw everything into mud. The huts the soldiers built kept them warm and sheltered from most of the harshest conditions. Valley Forge was not the worst winter the men of the Continental Army would endure, but it made them all the stronger for what was to come.

Several times during the winter, Henry appealed to Washington to let him form a partisan corps consisting of both infantry and cavalry. In other words, Henry was seeking to command his own brigade. It is probable he hoped that with the command would come the promotion to brigadier general he so desperately wanted. In December of 1777 his brother Robert had written to Washington suggesting a partisan corps for Henry (R. Livingston to Washington

December 8, 1777). In addition to the anticipated promotion, this would have had the advantage of allowing Henry to operate essentially on his own again. Independent command was where he had stood out over and over again. Yet Washington said no. He said bluntly that the army simply did not have the strength to give up men for the corps. He also suggested that Livingston could potentially be up for command of the light infantry corps that was coalescing but would be up against Daniel Morgan, the famed rifleman, and several others (Washington December 27, 1777). In short, Robert Livingston could not use his political influence to advance his brother's career in the army this time.

Henry was not discouraged in his push for an independent command. He wrote on January 22 that he would not recruit men from the army for his partisan corps but only use his own regiment and recruit horsemen from outside the army. He wanted to use the corps for "Annoying the Enemy by embracing all Opportunities of surprising, harassing and distressing them" (H. B. Livingston to Washington January 22, 1778).

This time Washington apparently agreed to meet with Henry about his idea. Although no record exists of exactly what was said at this meeting, after

Henry explained his idea for a partisan corps again, Washington said no, based on the expense of equipping the corps.

Henry made one more attempt to get Washington to authorize his partisan corps. From Pikeland Township, where Henry had removed to after falling ill, he wrote to Washington, finally admitting that raising a new cavalry corps would be expensive. Based on information that he got from a French cavalry officer, the corps would take at least a year to train to operate in conjunction with his infantry. So, he hoped to have a partisan corps just made up of infantry. Washington said no.

It is unclear what illness befell Henry, but it left him bedridden for weeks. Many, many soldiers in the Valley Forge camp became ill and many of them died from the illnesses. Henry had the advantage of being able to leave the camp when he fell ill and of being in the company of his regimental surgeon Dr. John Vascher, who was also ill but essentially acted as a personal doctor during Henry's illness (H. B. Livingston February 10, 1778).

Henry was back with his men at Valley Forge by March 25, 1778 when he wrote to Robert about the major developments and changes in the army. A "Prussian Lieutenant General arrived in camp, and knight of the Black Eagle &c which he wears made of lead tied to one of his buttonholes." This was of course Friedrich Wilhelm August Heinrich Ferdinand von Steuben, the Baron von Steuben. Henry described the new training the Baron was putting the army through as "more agreeable to the dictates of Reason and Commonsense than any mode I have before seen." The men were still working on marching where slow time was faster than they were used to, and quick time was "about as quick as a common Country Dance." Between his arrival in camp and the Americans breaking camp, von Steuben taught them how to be an army. Beginning with small groups of men and moving up to larger and larger groups until the whole army was drilling together, von Steuben taught the men how to march as one, load their muskets as one, and in general fight as one. All in the style of European armies of the time.

Henry was also a bit prescient in his letter, predicting that he would be put in command in one of the chosen regiments that would advance in front of the army. These regiments were to be made up of the best soldiers from all the regiments in the army to create crack regiments that would be the first to attack the British army. He was sure that this appointment would bring him "an acquisition of danger without the most distant prospect of acquiring Honor adequate" (H. B. Livingston to R. Livingston March 25,1778).

In March of 1778 Henry sent his enslaved man Jack to Robert to borrow seven and a half guineas hard cash in order to pay a debt to Dr. Vascher, who he was trying to have court martialed at the time. The money was owed for some stockings and fabric that had been smuggled out of Philadelphia. He found the debt to be an embarrassment (H. B. Livingston to R. Livingston March 25, 1778). The debt could also have been seen by the members of the court as a motivating factor for the court martial. They may have thought that Henry was attempting to court martial Vascher to get rid of him so that he would not have to pay the debt back.

Henry was finally successful in having Vascher court martialed on April 1. The charges were neglect of duty, disobedience of orders, conduct unbecoming an officer and a gentleman, using menacing language to his Colonel, and spreading false reports regarding his prejudice. The doctor was found not guilty and acquitted with full honor (Washington April 11, 1778).

Earlier, Henry had also court martialed his quartermaster, the officer in charge of regimental supplies, Peter Vonck. The charges against Vonck were neglect of duty and appropriating for his own use rum and soap drawn for the regiment. Vonck was found guilty. He was discharged from the army, forfeited all his pay—and his crime, name, and place of abode was to be published in papers in and around camp and in his home state. It was to be considered scandalous for an officer of the Continental Army to be associated with him. Vonck was utterly humiliated for his crimes both within the army and among his friends and neighbors. A First Lieutenant in the regiment, John Lloyd, was convicted of ungentlemanly behavior for advising and assisting Vonck with his crimes. He was believed to have taken a fair share of the misbegotten rum as well. He was sentenced to dismissal from the army (Washington March 24, 1778).

In addition to the failed court martial of Dr. Vascher in April, there is another piece of evidence that Henry was slipping into his quarrelsome ways while encamped at Valley Forge, even though he had the new training to focus on when he was not fighting. On March 24 Lieutenant Colonel Pierre Regnier wrote a letter directly to George Washington asking to be removed from the 4th New York regiment, either by transfer or discharge. He could no longer bear to be under the command of Henry Livingston. He described serving under Henry as "being obliged to live in a perpetual state of dissention, and be under the power of a man, whose unbounded Pride and thirst is to Tirranise [*sic*] and overpower, by his untractable [*sic*] humour—all those under his command" (Regnier 1778).

Whatever the quarrel between Regnier and Henry was, it led to yet another court martial. This one must have stung Henry a bit, as he had asked for Regnier to be made his lieutenant colonel and had used the political influence of his friends to make it happen. On March 23, the day before Regnier wrote his letter to Washington, he was court martialed for disobedience of orders and refusal to do duty when required by his superior officer in a style unbecoming an inferior officer. Regnier was found not guilty and acquitted with honor (Washington March 30, 1778). Regnier was neither discharged from the army nor removed from the regiment. He continued to serve in the regiment for years to come.

Clearly, the time in camp was beginning to wear on Henry. The lion inside him was beginning to stir and it was leading to quarrels with his fellow officers. Fortunately for Henry and the lion, the time to break camp was rapidly approaching.

Figure 1. Colonel Henry Beekman Livingston. Courtesy of private collection.

Figure 2. Chancellor Robert R. Livingston. Courtesy of New York Public Library.

Figure 3. Major General Richard Montgomery. Courtesy of Library of Congress.

Figure 4. Major General Philip Schuyler. Courtesy of Library of Congress.

Figure 5. Death of General Montgomery. Courtesy of Library of Congress.

Figure 6. John Jay. Courtesy of Library of Congress.

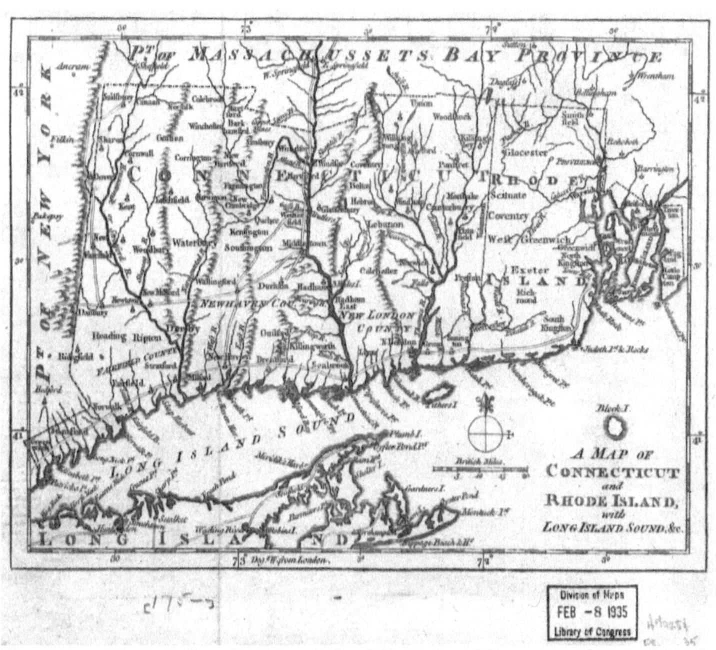

Figure 7. 1776 map showing Long Island Sound and the area of Long Island that Henry Beekman Livingston raided in 1776. Courtesy of Library of Congress.

Figure 8. Major General Oliver Delancey. Courtesy of Library of Congress.

Figure 9. Major General Alexander McDougall. Courtesy of New York Public Library.

Figure 10. Major General Israel Putnam. Courtesy of Library of Congress.

Figure 11. Major General Benedict Arnold. Courtesy of Library of Congress.

Figure 12. Surrender of General Burgoyne at Saratoga. Courtesy of Library of Congress

Figure 13. General Henry Clinton. Courtesy of Library of Congress.

Figure 14. General George Washington. Courtesy of Library of Congress

Figure 15. Valley Forge. Courtesy of Library of Congress.

Figure 16. Major General Baron von Steuben. Courtesy of Library of Congress

Figure 17. Major General Charles Lee. Courtesy Library of Congress

Figure 18. Major General Anthony Wayne. Courtesy of Library of Congress.

Figure 19. Major General John Sullivan. Courtesy of Library of Congress.

Figure 20. Major General The Marquis de La Fayette. Courtesy of Library of Congress.

Chapter Five

The Lion Roars

On June 18, 1778 the British army, now under the command of Henry's old nemesis, General Henry Clinton, abandoned Philadelphia, where they had spent the winter "rolling in the fat of the land, having played the soldier sufficiently to secure them the best quarters" (H. B. Livingston to R. Livingston December 24, 1777). But the entrance of the French into the war meant that it was possible the French fleet could have cut off Clinton's army in Philadelphia and waited for them to starve.

On June 19, 1778 the American army broke camp to pursue them, six months to the day they had marched into Valley Forge. Thanks to the training they had received from Baron von Steuben, the American army that pursed the British army was very different from the American army that had marched into camp the past winter nearly naked and with spirits at an all-time low. They were regular soldiers, trained in the European style, finally ready to face the British on equal footing.

As he predicted, Henry was given command of one of the battalions made up of chosen men from throughout the army. Command of the other two battalions was given to Colonel James Wesson and Colonel Walter Stewart. They were brigaded under the command of General Anthony Wayne. This brigade was part of a 4,500-man detachment under the command of Major General Charles Lee. (Stone 2017, 189–190).

Lee had been captured by the British on December 12, 1776 while sitting in a tavern complaining about George Washington's command. Lee felt that his experience in the British, Portuguese, and Polish armies had made him more qualified to lead the army than Washington. After sixteen months as a British prisoner, Lee had been released in a prisoner exchange. He was completely ignorant of how the army had changed in his absence and still believed it to consist of a rabble of militia rather than the well-trained army of regulars it had become under Washington and von Steuben. Lee now made it overtly clear that he thought he should command the army rather than Washington and thought the army should fight a defensive war rather than face the British in open battle.

Lee had at first refused the command of the measly 4,500-man vanguard, but when he saw Marie-Joseph Paul Yves Roch Gilbert du Motier, Marquis de La Fayette, leap at the chance to take command and begin to push the vanguard after the British, Lee changed his mind and took command.

On June 28 Lee caught the rearguard of the British army at Monmouth Court House, New Jersey. Henry's battalion were among the men ordered to advance directly at the enemy. Before they reached musket range of the enemy, the other American regiments began to fall back. British cannons began to rain cannonballs amongst the American soldiers. Henry retreated in fairly good order, his men stayed in line and did not break and run away but took many casualties in doing so. Among his casualties were Major Dickinson, who was killed by British fire, and Lieutenant Colonel Badlam, who, like many soldiers that day, fell to heat exhaustion. It has been speculated that the temperature rose above ninety degrees (H. B. Livingston to R. Livingston June 30, 1778).

As the main body of the army approached, George Washington found most of Lee's command in utter chaos. He chewed out Lee with language so strong that it was not recorded by any of his subordinates, and Lee believed he had been relieved of his command. Clinton was pouring more and more men from his army into the fray until the day had become a full-scale battle. At this point someone spotted Henry's battalion, fatigued and very thinned out from their retreat but still in good order, and commanded them to screen a battery of American cannons that were just being rolled into place. Who gave these orders became an issue of contention at Charles Lee's court martial and for historians in writing about the battle of Monmouth.

At Lee's court martial Alexander Hamilton claimed credit for giving the orders. While Lee countered that he had given the orders, Hamilton claimed not to have heard Lee issue any orders to that effect (Proceedings: Lee Court-Martial 1778). Some sources suggest that La Fayette had actually issued the orders because Washington had sent him to take command of Lee's disordered force and because of his presence with Henry's battalion in the ensuing action (Stone 2017, 306). Henry could have cleared this up, but he was not called to testify at the court martial, and in his letter on the battle to Robert Livingston he simply said that he had received orders to cover the artillery. Perhaps even to his brother, he was unwilling to say what had actually transpired that day in regard to the disorderly command structure. He dreaded being called as a witness to the court martial of Lee because he thought, "I can say nothing in his favour" (H. B. Livingston to R. Livingston June 30, 1778).

Regardless of who issued the orders, Henry led his much-beleaguered battalion to the cannons and then on to a hedgerow to the west. Here, Henry and his men exchanged extremely heavy musket fire with the British. Henry was struck by a musket ball in the thigh, which luckily traveled through without hitting the bone, but he refused to leave the field for treatment, aware that he was the last standing field officer in his battalion. He was unwilling to leave his men without someone to command them. It was not until the British were able to flank both sides of the hedgerow that Henry gave the order to retreat. But he had done his duty and given Washington the time to deploy the army to receive the main thrust of the British army. Henry wrote "Abt. this time Gen:l Washington Came up with the Rest of the Army and very soon Changed the Face of Affairs and beat the Enemy Back to their Ground" (H. B. Livingston to R. Livingston June 30, 1778). It was done. The American army had beaten the British army in a stand-up open field battle. At the end of the day, the British had retreated and the Americans had held their ground.

It had cost him a musket ball through the leg and a third of his battalion, but Henry's lion had roared, and he received accolades for it. Washington's secretary thought Henry had been very powerful in his fire (Stone 2017, 313). John Laurens wrote to his father that Henry deserved well of his country and had distinguished himself nobly (Rhodehamel 2001). Alexander Hamilton said that Henry had behaved "very handsomely" (Hamilton 1778). Perhaps the most important accolade, at least to Henry, came immediately after the battle. With his assembled battalion mostly dispersed back to their home regiments and his leg bandaged, Henry was given temporary command of General Enoch Poor's brigade. The lion inside Henry was ready for more fighting but would be frustrated by the British retreat. Henry wrote, "I was Honour'd with the Command of Gen:l Poors Brigade but unfortunately it did not come to Action or I should have taken ample Revenge" (H. B. Livingston to R. Livingston June 30, 1778). Perhaps he was talking about revenge for his leg, or perhaps he was talking about revenge for all his men who had not been able to walk off the field of battle that day—or perhaps both, his thoughts once again focused on both himself and his men.

After a short time to recuperate, Henry was thrown right back into the thick of the fighting in

Rhode Island. When Henry heard about the possibility of a fight while on furlough in Rhode Island on personal business, he showed up at General John Sullivan's camp. Sullivan gave him command of his light corps of infantry, much to the chagrin of other officers, including James and William Livingston, who did not understand by what right Henry was even with the army at Rhode Island (Bigelow et al. 1778). Other officers, including General Nathanael Greene and the Marquis de La Fayette, had been sent by George Washington to Rhode Island to bolster General Sullivan's officer corps, while Henry had shown up of his own accord (McBurney 2018).

For his part, Henry was happy to be away from his regiment. The 4th New York Regiment was encamped at White Plains, New York. Once again, they were under the command of Alexander McDougall. In a letter to his brother Henry quipped, "you know the affection we bear each other" (H. B. Livingston to R. LivingstonAugust 8, 1778). Time had done little to smooth over the acrimony between the two men.

In Rhode Island, Sullivan was laying siege to British troops in Newport on Aquidneck Island. The British had taken Newport in 1776 in an attack led by General Henry Clinton and had held it ever since. Sullivan had been sent to take it back with a single attack but was unable to due to British raids on his supply depots. Instead, he invested the town in a siege. Newport was then chosen to be the first place that American and French forces would cooperate during the war.

The French had entered the war on the side of the Americans on February 6, 1778. Prior to their official alliance, the French had been supplying weapons and other necessities of war to the Americans via smugglers. Following their official announcement of alliance and declaration of war on England, the French were able to openly turn their army and navy on the British. Hundreds of ships and thousands of soldiers would be sent over to aid the American cause. The alliance also turned the war into a world war, as both the British and French had territories all over the world that they would have to protect from one another. When word of the alliance reached Valley Forge, General Washington ordered a celebration. The army fired a feu de joie, cheered the King of France, and received an extra ration of rum that evening. Henry, to celebrate the alliance, received permission to redesign the uniform of the 4th New York Regiment into a style more similar to French uniforms. The 4th New York Regiment would wear white coats with red facings.

The fact that the French would be joining the fight in Rhode Island had led to the turnout of thousands of militia men from Rhode Island, Massachusetts, and New Hampshire. On August 9, Jean Baptiste Charles Henri Hector, comte d'Estaing landed 4,000 French troops on the island, who immediately began digging in. On August 22, following a major storm that damaged several ships of the French and British fleets and skirmishing between French and British ships as they sought their own scattered fleets—the French fleet, including their troops investing Newport, retreated to Boston. The abandonment by the French led to mass desertions by the militia and a severe blow to the morale of the Continental regulars stationed at Rhode Island. By August 28 Sullivan realized that holding his position had become untenable. He decided to abandon the island the next day, and word got to the British, who decided to attack while the Americans were in the vulnerable position of retreating.

The American forces were divided into two parts. On the right, General Nathanael Greene commanded, and on the left General John Glover commanded. Henry was stationed about two miles in front of Glover's main line, commanding a group of light infantry troops who were used to moving fast and skirmishing. British General Francis Smith was sent with two entire regiments to attack the left wing of the American army. They found Henry in their way. Henry's men opened fire with such ferocity that the two regiments they faced could not advance and had to fall back. They called for reinforcements and forced Henry to retreat to Quaker Hill. Seeing that that hill was in danger of being flanked, Henry retreated to the main American line.

The British next attacked the American right side under the command of Greene. The fighting was intense, and Henry was sent from the left side of the American lines to the right to support Greene's forces. The British were fighting from behind a stone wall. Greene ordered him to attack the flank of the enemy, which was protected by a group of Hessians. Henry led his men with his sword drawn and their bayonets fixed. Under fire from cannons in a redoubt behind the British lines and from two British ships offshore, Henry led his men into the thick of the fighting. The light infantry fought so hard they were able to dislodge the British and Hessians from behind their stone wall. The British retreated up the prosaically named Turkey Hill. Greene's forces moved to hold the stone wall below the hill. In the melee Henry was grazed by a musket ball in the elbow but dismissed the wound as too minor to be concerned about (H. B. Livingston to R. Livingston August 31, 1778).

The Americans withdrew in an orderly fashion

the next day without molestation by the British. Henry was one of the last officers to leave the island (McBurney 2018, 185, 191, 201). Sullivan would write to Congress that Henry and the officers of the light corps had behaved with remarkable spirit (E. B. Livingston 1998, 247). In his report to George Washington, Nathanael Greene made it a point to mention Henry's skirmishing with the head of the British column and mentioned him among the officers who had "done themselves great honor in the transactions of the day" (Greene 1778).

The lion had roared for the last time. With no clear enemy to fight and with his regiment stationed in New York, Henry became quarrelsome once again. Soon that quarrelsome part of his nature would drive him out of the army.

Chapter Six

The Lion Withers

THROUGHOUT THE WAR Henry had been concerned with his rank in the army. He worried constantly about his rank but also about his seniority, where he competed with other officers of his own rank. This stems from his desire not to serve under men he considered inferior, which included men of lesser breeding as well as men of lesser military skill and experience. Henry was an aristocrat by birth despite his roughness and had become something of a military aristocrat by his experience. There were few men in the army whom Henry judged worthy by birth or by experience to command him.

Even in the early days of the war, Henry was surprised that the original commission he received was not higher than that of a captain. He had served as a major in the colonial militia before the war (New York State Legislature 1842, 2:28). The dispute with

McDougall and Putnam in 1777 was the result of disagreement over ranks. Henry felt that McDougall was a lesser man than he was, and he felt that he should be senior to Van Cortlandt when assigned to his command. In his letter to George Washington of January 22,1778 in which he requested command of a partisan corps, Henry began the letter by complaining about rank. He wrote, "it May one Day fall to my Lott to be commanded by those Formerly my Inferiors in Rank and not entitled to this superiority by their past Experience or the possession of any extraordinary Military Merit." On the other hand, he was hesitant to resign while "Tyranny is extending ruin And devastation" (H. B. Livingston to Washington January 22, 1778). The Committee of Arrangement, which was supposed to handle issues of rank and seniority, was so confused by the issue of seniority among New York's colonels that they wrote to George Clinton to explain it to the best of his ability (Smith 1983, 10:511–512). Evidently, Henry was not happy with Clinton's answer to this letter.

Ultimately, the lack of promotion overwhelmed Henry's sense of duty, and he chose to resign from the army. He tried to resign directly to George Washington, but the general would not accept his commission and sent him to Congress. He then sent his commission to Henry Laurens to give to

Congress. Though he liked to serve, he was not "insensible of the repeated indignities offered me in the promotion of officers my inferior in the army to superior rank." Continuing in the army would be "incompatible with the preservation of my reputation and honor" (H. B. Livingston to R. Livingston November 19, 1778). James Duane wrote to Robert Livingston that Henry's reputation in Congress was high, and they were reluctant to let him resign. Duane appealed to Henry to serve one more campaign season, but Henry simply could not. The New York State legislature, on the other hand, seemed indifferent about his resignation. Duane wrote that Henry must accept "the truth of the maxim that a prophet has no honor in his own country."

In this letter from Duane there is also a small hint of something else that might have been driving Henry at this particular time. Henry had left Philadelphia before his resignation was officially accepted by Congress to travel to New Jersey where he was to meet a Miss Rutherford and "put an end to long courtship by a happy marriage." Henry was now twenty-eight years old and had spent the last four years of his life fighting in some of the most brutal battles on American soil and living the hard life of a soldier in camp. He had been nearly frozen during campaigns, had been laid low for weeks with an illness that could have claimed his life, and had been wounded at least twice in battle. It seems that Henry was thinking of starting a family and settling down (Smith 1985, 11:400–401).

For reasons lost to history, Henry and Miss Rutherford were not married. Henry must have been heartbroken, for he considered fleeing the country. Henry wrote to an unnamed officer on April 11, 1779, most likely Benedict Arnold, for a certificate of his service at Saratoga as he had "views of serving abroad" (H. B. Livingston-NYS Archives April 11, 1779). On May 20, 1779 he received a certificate from George Washington noting he had served as a captain, lieutenant colonel, and colonel with command of a regiment. He also paid Henry a great compliment by saying he had always "maintained the character of an intelligent, active & brave Officer, having distinguished himself upon several occasions" (Washington 1779).

Henry decided not to look for fights overseas but instead retired to his home at Rhinebeck, which he had inherited from his grandfather, Colonel Henry Beekman. He ventured out once more in October of 1780 at the head of a group of levies, essentially a drafted militia. It was somewhat ignominious, in that his group of levies were charged with carrying supplies to Fort Herkimer rather than with any combat role. The closest they came to combat was when a dispatch rider from George Clinton mistook the pickets that Henry had set out for loyalist militia and threw away his messages. Once he was caught and calmed down, a search could not turn up the lost messages. At the end of this mini campaign Henry did sit on the court martial board for three spies but soon returned home without any new laurels to hang on his mantle (Clinton 1902, 6:317–318, 334).

Despite his resignation Henry remained friendly with George Washington. In 1782, when Washington toured the Northern Department, he left his wife Martha with Henry's mother Margaret Beekman Livingston at Clermont. On his return to Clermont, Washington made it a point to visit Henry at his home for a few hours before heading back to his headquarters at Newburgh.

In May 1783 Henry wrote to George Washington about one of his tenants, Richard Dickinson, who was tricked into getting drunk and enlisting in Colonel Marinus Willet's regiment of state levies. This was problematic because he was a member of the Saratoga Convention Army, the British soldiers surrendered by Burgoyne after his loss at Saratoga, and he faced immediate execution should he be captured by the British. In addition, Dickinson had a young family who desperately needed him (H. B.

Livingston to Washington 1783). Washington wrote back that he would have the man discharged if there was any impropriety in his recruitment into the levies (Washington 1783).

Henry did not have a tremendously successful life after his time in the army. He was married to Anne Hume Shippen, a well-known Philadelphia socialite and cousin to Benedict Arnold's wife, but after producing one child, the marriage fell apart. Anne—or Nancy, as she was known—returned to her family's home in Philadelphia while Henry remained in New York. The marriage eventually ended when Henry was able to obtain a divorce on the grounds that she abandoned him. His brother Robert had used his influence to block the divorce in New York, so Henry had to move to Connecticut briefly to obtain the divorce. He had three other children with another woman, Maria Van Klief, whom he never married, making them illegitimate under the law. These two events caused a rift between Henry and his mother and brother, Robert. Though he was still welcome at the homes of a few of his sisters and their husbands, he was never welcome back at Clermont.

He was often in financial trouble. On November 23, 1782 he wrote to his brother Robert for a loan of "one or two hundred pounds" (H. B. Livingston 1782). In 1789 he, like many other men, wrote to

Washington seeking a compensation for his time in the army, or a job. He wrote "My Confidence in America while Struggling for Freedom, has reduced me to Poverty" (H. B. Livingston to Washington June 12, 1789). The money his father had left him, and the value of the land he had sold had been destroyed by the inflation of Continental currency. He even considered moving to the Mississippi River to see if his prospects were better there. He remained at his home, though.

In 1804 Henry was once again in need of money. He offered his stock of cows, calves, horses, sheep, and bulls for sale. If he was unable to find a buyer, he would auction the animals off at a nearby hotel (H. B. Livingston 1804).

In January 1809 he wrote to President Thomas Jefferson. He sought a commission in the army for his son, John B. Livingston, one of his illegitimate children. John was educated and had become a lawyer under Henry's supervision but desired a post in the army like his father. Henry also took the opportunity of this letter to ask for a commission for himself as well. He had come to regret what he called "the unpardonable Crime of Resignation." He expressed a fear of dying impoverished like many other former officers of the Revolution and claimed he was willing not only to command but to obey, a change from his more quarrelsome days as a younger man (H. B. Livingston 1809). Thomas Jefferson was out of office within a matter of weeks, and no commission came either for Henry or for John. Perhaps his reputation as a quarrelsome officer in camp with no enemy to fight at the time outweighed his reputed skill in battle.

The Marquis de La Fayette made his grand return to America in 1824. While being carried up the Hudson River from fete to fete on a steamboat, the Marquis was stopped by an old man who had had himself rowed out into the river. Henry climbed aboard the steamboat for an emotional reunion with his comrade whom he had fought next to at Monmouth and Rhode Island. After the visit Henry was rowed back to shore and the Marquis' steamboat carried on to its next stop, Clermont. Henry had not been invited to the party there (Brandt 1986, 167–168).

With no further opportunities to fight for his nation, Henry seemed to wither on the vine. He cared for his illegitimate children, including one who had a mental disability, but he was not the lion he had once been.

Henry passed away at his house in Rhinebeck on November 6, 1831. He died intestate, and according to Dutchess County Surrogate Court records, his real estate had to be sold to pay his debts. John

Armstrong Jr., husband of Henry's sister Alida, acted as administrator of the estate.

A simple death notice ran in the *Albany Argus* newspaper: "Died, At his residence in Rhinebeck, on the 6th inst. Colonel HENRY B. LIVINGSTON, aged 81 years, a patriot of the revolution and brother of the present Secretary of State" (*Albany Argus* 1831). He was buried in a tomb belonging to his brother-in-law, Thomas Tillotson, at the Rhinebeck Reformed Church. A memorial stone stands in the church yard, but the location of his remains has been lost to time. A fitting end to a man who burned brilliantly for a few years and then faded away.

Epilogue

PERHAPS HENRY BEEKMAN Livingston was a soldier for another time. Perhaps he was better suited to some ancient battlefield where his ability to lead men into a fight would be all he would need to receive honor and accolades. Unfortunately, he was born in a time when a soldier had to be a warrior, a gentleman, and a politician.

Which is not to say that Henry wasn't a gentleman. Far from it, in fact. He had been raised into one of the most important families in the colony of New York. He would have been familiar from a very early age with which fork to use when, how to dance the right dances, and how to navigate the very inviolable social order of things.

It was this understanding of the social order that led to Henry's reputation for being quarrelsome. He truly believed that he was better than many other people and that his very being entitled him to more than those lesser born. Combined with his successes on the various battlefields of the war, his ego demanded nothing less than higher rank.

Barring that, Henry had no choice but to resign from the army—a mistake, he later realized—nevertheless, his honor demanded it at the time. On the battlefields of Long Island, Saratoga, Monmouth, and Rhode Island—Henry had served with honor and distinction but could never grasp that next ring he was always reaching for.

Henry's end was sad. He had separated from his wife and, by her choice, been put aside by his daughter from that marriage. He had other children whom he cared for, but they were not able to live a consistently comfortable life because of Henry's money troubles. They could not even count on the pension Henry had earned from his service during the war, because it could only go to his legitimate child, and she was not inclined to share.

Ultimately, Henry's story has the makings of a Greek tragedy wherein the hero is brought low by his own hubris. Sadly, Henry sought, but never got, his redemption arc. His hubris did not wane until it was too late for him to make good on many aspects of his life. Too many friends and family had died or scattered to the winds, and his enemies were too many to number.

When Henry died, he was all but a broken man.

He had failed at civilian life. The one thing he truly excelled at was leading men into battle, and after 1778 he was never able to do that again. He died like an old lion in a zoo—far from the young patriot, as brave as could be imagined, who had roared across battlefields decades earlier.

Index

Bibliography

Albany Argus. 1831. “Died.” November 18,2

Bigelow, Timothy. 1778. “Petition to General Sullivan.” Robert R. Livingston Papers. August 18.

Brandt, Clare. 1986. *An American Aristocracy: The Livingstons*. New York: Doubleday & Company.

Clinton, George. 1900. Public Papers of George Clinton First Governor of New York 1775-1795-1801-1804. Vol. 2. New York: The State of New York.

Clinton, George. 1902. Public Papers of George Clinton, First Governor of New York 1777-1795-1801-1804. Vol. 6. New York: State of New York.

Convention of New York. 1776. “Letter from the Convention of New York to the Committees of East and South Hampton.” Northern Illinois University Digital Library. July 19. Accessed May 24, 2020. https:/digital.lib.niu.edu/islandora/onject/niu-amarch%3A97692.

Dangerfield, George. 1960. *Chancellor Robert R. Livingston of New York 1746-1813*. New York: Harcourt Brace & Company.

Delafield, Maturin L. 1889. "Henry Beekman Livingston to his Father 6 October 1775." Edited by Mrs. Martha J. Lamb. *Magazine of American History* with Notes and Queries XXI: 256–258.

Greene, Nathanael. 1778. "To George Washington from Major General Nathanael Greene, 28–31 August 1778." Founders Online. Accessed May 12, 2020. https://founders.archives.gov/documents/Washington/03-16-02-0439.

Hamilton, Alexander. 1778. "From Alexander Hamilton to Elias Boudinot, [5 July 1778]." Founders Online. Accessed May 12, 2020. https://founders.archives.gov/documents/Hamilton/01-01-02-0499.

———. 1777. "From Alexander Hamilton to George Washington, 15 November 1777." Founders Online. Accessed May 12, 2020. https://founders.archives.gov/documents/Hamilton/01-01-02-0343.

Hay, Ann Hawkes. 1777. "To George Washington from Colonel Ann Hawkes Hay, 23 March 1777." Founders Online. Accessed May 12, 2020. https://founders.archives.gov/documents/Washington/03-08-02-0670.

Jay, John. 1777. "From George Washington to John Jay, 20 February 1777." Founders Online. Accessed May 12, 2020. https://founders.archives.gov/documents/Washington/03-08-02-0417.

Lender, Mark Edward, and Gary Wheeler Stone. 2017. *Fatal Sunday: George Washington, the Monmouth Campaign and the Politics of Battle.* Norman, OK: University of Oklahoma Press.

Livingston, Edwin Brockholst. 1998. *The Livingstons of Livingston Manor*. Milwaukee: Curtis House.

Livingston, Henry Beekman. n.d. "Account Book." Collection of the Columbia County Historical Society.

Livingston, Henry Beekman. 1775. "Capt. Henry B. Livingston to the New York Congress." American Archives Northern Illinois University Digital Library. June 6. Accessed May 20, 2020. https://digital.lib.niu.edu/islandora/object/niu-amarch%3A82244

———. 1775. "Capt. Henry B. Livingston to New York Congress." American Archives Northern Illinois University Digital Library. August 8. Accessed May 20, 2020. https://digital.lib.niu.edu/islandora/object/niu-amarch%3A95527.

———. 1775. "Capt. Henry B. Livingston to New York Congress." American Archives Northern Illinois University Digital Library. August 8.

Accessed May 20, 2020. https://digital.lib.niu.edu/islandora/object/niu-amarch%3A95527.

Livingston, Robert R. 1775. Manuscript and Archives Division-New York Public Library Digital Collection. November 14. Accessed January 5, 2021. https:/digitalcollections.nypl.org/items/94479130-fdd3-0133-0886-00505686a51c.

———. 1776. "To George Washington from Lieutenant Colonel Henry Beekman Livingston, 14 May 1776." Founders Online Accessed July 29, 2020. https://founders.archives.gov/documents/Washington/03-04-02-0238.

———. 1776. "To George Washington from Lieutenant Colonel Henry Beekman Livingston, 21 May 1776." Founders Online. Accessed July 29, 2020. https://founders.archives.gov/documents/Washington/03-04-02-0291.

———. 1776. "To George Washington from Lieutenant Colonel Henry Beekman Livingston, July 1776." Founders Online. Accessed December 13, 2020. https://founders.archives.gov/documents/Washington/03-05-02-0395.

———. 1776. "Henry Beekman Livingston to Robert R. Livingston." Robert R. Livingston Papers. August 21.

———. 1776. "Letter from Governor Trumbull to General Washington." [Letter from HBL to

Trumbull, subsequently forwarded to George Washington.] Northern Illinois University Digital Library. August 30. Accessed May 24, 2020. https://digital,lib.niu.edu/islandora/object/niu-amarch%3A81276.

———. 1776. "Henry Beekman Livingston to Robert R. Livingston." Robert R. Livingston Papers. September

———. 1776. "Letter from Colonel Livingston to Governor Trumbull: The people of East and South Hampton have almost universally taken an oath of allegiance to the King." Northern Illinois University Digital Library. September 4. Accessed May 20, 2020. https://digital.lib.niu.edu/islandora/object/niu-amarch%3A93879.

———. 1776. "Letter from Colonel Livingston to Governor Trumbull: He has taken Colonel Abram Gardiner, who tendered the oath of allegiance to the inhabitants." Northern Illinois University Digital Library. September 10. Accessed May 2020, 2020. https://digital.lib.niu.edu/islandora/object/niu-march%3A86589.

———. 1776. "To George Washington from Lieutenant Colonel Henry Beekman Livingston, 11 September 1776." Founders Online. Accessed May 12, 2020. https://founders.archives.gov/documents/Washington/03-06-02-0226.

———. 1776. "To George Washington from Lieutenant Colonel Henry Beekman Livingston, 11–14 June 1776." Founders Online. Accessed July 29, 2020. https://founders.archives.gov/documents/Washington/03-04-02-0393.

———. 1776. "To George Washington from Lieutenant Colonel Henry Beekman Livingston, 30 August 1776." Founders Online. Accessed December 13, 2020. https://founders.archives.gov/documents/Washington/03-06-02-0140.

———. 1776. "To George Washington from Lieutenant Colonel Henry Beekman Livingston, 31 August 1776." Founders Online. Accessed May 12, 2020. https://founders.archives.gov/documents/Washington/03-06-02-0150.

———. 1776. "Letter from Colonel Livingston to the Connecticut Council of Safety: Has not succeeded in his determination to prevent the inhabitants of East Hampton supplying the Ministerial troops with livestock." Northern Illinois University Digital Library. September 7. Accessed May 20, 2020. https://digital.lib.niu.edu/islandora/object/niu-amarch%3A87090.

———. 1776. "Letter from Colonel Henry B. Livingston to Governor Trumbull: A most infamous abettor of the Ministry is just now brought in—one Zeb Howell." Northern Illinois

University Digital Library. September 15. Accessed May 20, 2020. https://digital.lib.niu.edu/islandora/object/niu-amarch%3A86484.

———. 1776. "Henry Beekman Livingston to Robert R. Livingston." Robert R. Livingston Papers. September 24.

———. 1776. "To George Washington from Lieutenant Colonel Henry Beekman Livingston, 24 September 1776." Founders Online. Accessed May 12, 2020. https://founders.archives.gov/documents/Washington/03-06-02-0302.

———. 1776. "Colonel Livingston to New York Committee of Arrangement." Northern Illinois University Digital Library. November 26. Accessed May 29, 2020. https://digital.lib.niu/islandora/object/niu-amarch3A101127.

———. 1777. "To George Washington from Colonel Henry Beekman Livingston, 7 March 1777." Founders Online. Accessed May 12, 2020. https://founders.archives.gov/documents/Washington/03-08-02-0561

———. 1777. "To George Washington from Colonel Henry Beekman Livingston, 12 March 1777." Founders Online. Accessed May 12, 2020. https://founders.archives.gov/documents/Washington/03-08-02-0592.

———. 1777. "To George Washington from Colonel

Henry Beekman Livingston, 29 March 1777." Founders Online. Accessed May 12, 2020. https://founders.archives.gov/documents/Washington/03-09-02-0017.

———. 1777. "To George Washington from Colonel Henry Beekman Livingston, 19 May 1777." Founders online. Accessed May 12, 2020. https://founders.archives.gov/documents/Washington/03-09-02-0468.

———. 1777. "Henry Beekman Livingston to Robert R. Livingston." Robert R. Livingston Papers. June 30.

———. 1777. "Henry Beekman Livingston to Robert R. Livingston." Robert R. Livingston Papers. October 4.

———. 1777. "Henry Beekman Livingston to Robert R. Livingston." Robert R. Livingston Papers. October 10.

———. 1777. "Henry Beekman Livingston to Robert R. Livingston." Robert R. Livingston Papers. October 14.

———. 1777. "Henry Beekman Livingston to General Henry Clinton." Robert R. Livingston Papers. October 31. Accessed December 16, 2020. http://clermontstatehistoricsite.blogspot.com/2011/08/calamities-of-war-part-4.html

———. 1777. "Henry Beekman Livingston to Robert

R. Livingston." Robert R. Livingston Papers. November 30.

———. 1777. "Henry Beekman Livingston to Governor George Clinton." Collections of the New York State Archives, Henry Livingston Collection. November 13.

———. 1777. "To George Washington from Robert R. Livingston, 8 December 1777." Founders Online. Accessed May 5, 2020. https://founders.archives.gov/documents/Washington/03-12-02-0527.

———. 1777. "Henry Beekman Livingston to Robert R. Livingston." Robert R. Livingston Papers. Vol. 2. Edited by Joseph Boyle. December 24.

———. 1778. "To George Washington from Colonel Henry Beekman Livingston, 22 January 1778." Founders Online. Accessed May 12, 2020. https://founders.archives.gov/documents/Washington/03-13-02-0273

--------. 1778. "To George Washington from Colonel Henry Beekman Livingston, 10 February 1778." Founders Online. Accessed May 12, 2020. https://founders.archives.gov/documents/Washington/03-13-02-0417

———. 1778. "Henry Beekman Livingston to Robert R. Livingston." Rutgers University, Alexander

Library, Special Collections & Archives ACC. 3097. June 31.

———. 1778. "Henry Beekman Livingston to Robert R. Livingston." Robert R. Livingston Papers. August 8.

———. 1778. "Henry Beekman Livingston to Robert R. Livingston." Robert R. Livingston Papers. August 31.

———. 1778. "Henry Beekman Livingston to Robert R. Livingston." Robert R. Livingston Papers. November 19.

———. 1779. New York State Archives Henry Livingston Papers. April 11.

———. 1782. "Gilder Lehrman Collection GLC03107.03463." November 23.

———. 1783. "To George Washington from Henry Beekman Livingston, 26 May 1783." Founders Online Accessed May 12, 2020. https://founders.archives.gov/documents/Washington/99-01-02-11328

———. 1789. "To George Washington from Henry Beekman Livingston, 12 June 1789." Founders Online Accessed May 12, 2020. https://founders.archives.gov/documents/Washington/05-02-02-0348.

———. 1804. "For Sale." *Kingston New York Plebian*, August 12.

———. 1809. "To Thomas Jefferson from Henry Beekman Livingston, 15 January 1809." Founders Online. Accessed May 12, 2020. https://founders.archives.gov/documents/Jefferson/99-01-02-9546.

Louisiana Gazette. 1810. "Pierre Regnier's obituary from the *Louisiana Gazette*." June 6. Accessed December 14, 2020. https://louisianadigitallibrary.org/islandora/object/state-lwp%3A7743.

Luzander, John F. 2008. *Saratoga: A Military History of the Decisive Campaign of the American Revolution*. New York: Savas Beatie.

Mather, Frederic Gregory. 2010. *The Refugees of 1776 from Long Island to Connecticut*. Westminster, MD: Heritage Books.

McBurney, Christian M. 2018. *The Rhode Island Campaign: The First French and American Operation in the American Revolution*. Yardley, PA: Westholme Publishing.

McDougall, Alexander. 1777. "To George Washington from Brigadier General Alexander McDougall, 29 March 1777." Founders Online. Accessed May 12, 2020. https://founders.archives.gov/documents/Washington/03-09-02-0018.

New York Legislature 1842. Journals of the Provincial Congress, Provincial Convention, Committee of Safety and Council of Safety of the State of New York 1775-1776-1777. Vol. 2. Albany: New York State.

Proceedings: Lee Court-Martial 1778. "Proceedings of a General Court-Martial for the Trial of Major General Charles Lee, [13 July 1778]." Founders Online. July 13. Accessed May 12, 2020. https://founders.archives.gov/documents/Hamilton/01-01-02-0505.

Putnam, Israel. 1777. "To George Washington from Major General Israel Putnam, 10 June 1777." Founders Online. June 10. Accessed May 12, 2020. https://founders.archives.gov/documents/Washington/03-09-02-0660.

———. 1777. "To George Washington from Major General Israel Putnam, 9 June 1777." Founders Online. June 9. Accessed May 12, 2020. https://founders.archives.gov/documents/Washington/03-09-02-0650.

Regnier, Pierre. 1778. "To George Washington from Lieutenant Colonel Pierre Regnier de Roussi, 24 March 1778." Founders online. Accessed May 12, 2020. https://founders.archives.gov/documents/Washington/03-14-02-0268.

Rhodehamel, John, ed. 2001. *The American Revolution: Writings from the War of Independence.* New York: Library of America.

Roe, Daniel. 1904. *The Diary of Captain Daniel Roe.*

Edited by Alfred Seelye Roe. Worcester, MA: The Blanchard Press.

Sabine, W. H. W. 1954. *Suppressed History of General Nathaniel Woodhull*. New York: Colburn & Tegg.

Smith, Paul H., ed. 1977. Letters of Delegates to Congress. Vol. 2. Washington DC: Library of Congress.

———. 1985. Letters of Delegates to Congress. Vol. 11. Washington DC: Library of Congress.

———. 1983. Letters of Delegates to Congress. Vol. 10. Washington DC: Library of Congress.

Stirling, Lord. 1776. "To George Washington from Lord Stirling, 1 June 1776." Founders Online. Accessed July 29, 2020. https://founders.archives.gov/documents/Washington/03-04-02-0336.

Trumbull, Jonathan. 1776. "Letter from Governour Trumbull to Colonel Livingston." Northern Illinois University Digital Library. October 13. Accessed May 20, 2020. https://digital.lib.niu.edu/islandora/object/niu-amarch%3A98505.

Washington, George. 1776. "Orders to Colonel James Clinton, 14 June 1776." Founders Online. Accessed December 13, 2020. https://founders.archives.gov/documents/Washington/03-04-02-0409.

———. 1776. "From George Washington to

Lieutenant Colonel Henry Beekman Livingston, 4 May 1776." Founders Online. Accessed July 29, 2020. https://founders.archives.gov/documents/Washington/03-04-02-0166.

———. 1776. "From George Washington to Lieutenant Colonel Henry Beekman Livingston, 4 September 1776." Founders Online. Accessed May 12, 2020. —https://founders.archives.gov/documents/Washington/03-06-02-0176.

———. 1777. "From George Washington to Colonel Henry Beekman Livingston, 1 June 1777." Founders Online. Accessed May 12, 2020. https://founders.archives.gov/documents/Washington/03-09-02-0576.

———. 1777. "From George Washington to Colonel Henry Beekman Livingston, 20 February 1777." Founders Online. Accessed May 12, 2020. https://founders.archives.gov/documents/Washington/03-08-02-0418.

———. 1777. "From George Washington to Robert R. Livingston, 27 December 1777." Founders Online. Accessed May 12, 2020. https://founders.archives.gov/documents/Washington/03-13-02-0017.

———. 1778. "General Orders, 11 April 1778." Founders Online. Accessed May 12, 2020.

https://founders.archives.gov/documents/Washington/03-14-02-0439

———. 1778. "General Orders, 24 March 1778." Founders Online. March 24. Accessed May 12, 2020. https://founders.archives.gov/documents/Washington/03-14-02-0258.

———. 1778. "General Orders, 30 March 1778." Founders Online. March 30. Accessed December 29, 2020. https://founders.archives.gov/documents/Washington/03-14-02-0332

———. 1779. "Certificate for Henry Beekman Livingston, 20 May 1779." Founders Online. Accessed May 12, 2020. https://founders.archives.gov/documents/Washington/03-20-02-0491.

———. 1783. "From George Washington to Henry Beekman Livingston, 29 May 1783." Founders Online. May 29. Accessed May 12, 2020. https://founders.archives.gov/documents/Washington/99-01-02-11344.

Woodhull, Nathaniel. 1776. "To George Washington from Nathaniel Woodhull, 20 July 1776." Founders Online. July 20. Accessed December 13, 2020. https://founders.archives.gov/documents/Washington/03-05-02-0299.

Acknowledgments

First and foremost, I thank my wife Ashley, who supports me through all of my efforts, whether they pan out or not. My gratitude goes out, as well, to the rest of my family and friends, who endure my constant historic babbling as I work out my writing plans aloud—or give me a thumbs-up text when I dig up some little tidbit of information that excites me. I'd also like to thank all of the various institutions who have digitized letters and other information that allow a researcher like me to search a much broader range of sources than would normally be possible. And, to the authors whose books were also such invaluable sources—I stand on your shoulders. Finally, I fervently thank Henry Beekman Livingston for leaving me enough breadcrumbs to follow his path.

About the Author

Geoff Benton is the Curator of Collections and Education at Clermont State Historic Site. He received a BA in History and Biology at State University of New York (SUNY)/Potsdam and an MA in American History at SUNY/Albany. His previous works include *The Fight for Tom Cod: Newfoundland in the American Revolution*, *The Kinderhook Reformed Church: 300 Years of Faith and Community*, many articles in the *Columbia County History and Heritage* magazine, and a short essay on Henry Beekman Livingston in the *Journal of the American Revolution*. He lives in upstate New York with his very patient wife and reader Ashley and their two children. When not working or writing he is often found playing with his children or catching a baseball game in person or on TV.

www.ingramcontent.com/pod-product-compliance
Lightning Source LLC
LaVergne TN
LVHW091003080826
845145LV00003B/1110

* 9 7 8 1 9 5 4 7 4 4 3 6 3 *